I Like Sports

What Can I Be?

by Muriel L. Dubois

Consultant:
Barbara M. Parramore
Professor Emeritus, Curriculum and Instruction
North Carolina State University

Bridgestone Books
an imprint of Capstone Press
Mankato, Minnesota

Bridgestone Books are published by Capstone Press
151 Good Counsel Drive, P.O. Box 669, Mankato, Minnesota 56002
http://www.capstone-press.com

Library of Congress Cataloging-in-Publication Data
Dubois, Muriel L.
 I like sports: what can I be?/Muriel L. Dubois.
 p. cm.—(What can I be?)
 Includes bibliographical references (p.24) and index.
 Summary: Briefly describes some careers for people who enjoy sports, such as
professional athlete, coach, referee, sports broadcaster, and athletic trainer.
 ISBN 0-7368-0633-4
 1. Sports—Vocational guidance—Juvenile literature. [1. Sports—Vocational guidance.
2. Occupations.] I. Title. II. Series.
GV734.3 .D82 2001
796'.023'73—dc21
                 00-021375

Editorial Credits

Tom Adamson, editor; Heather Kindseth, designer; Katy Kudela, photo researcher

Photo Credits

Allan Laidman/Pictor, 14
Cheryl A. Ertelt, 10
Gene Lower, 12
Matt Swinden, 20
Michael Krasowitz/FPG International LLC, 6
Photo Network/Esbin-Anderson, 4
Photophile/Mark E. Gibson, cover (middle inset); Paul H. Henning, cover (top inset)
Pictor, cover (bottom inset)
Surgi Stock/FPG International LLC, 8
Tom Stodola, 16
Unicorn Stock Photos/Dick Young, cover; Mike Morris, 18

1 2 3 4 5 6 06 05 04 03 02 01

Table of Contents

People Who Enjoy Sports

You may like to be active. You may like to play a sport with your friends. Maybe you play on a team or like to watch sports. You can have a job in sports when you grow up.

Physical Education Teacher

Physical education teachers work in schools. They teach students how to play games. They teach the rules of sports. Physical education teachers help their students stay active and healthy.

Fitness Instructor

Fitness instructors show people how to stay in shape. Some instructors lead exercise groups. Other instructors show people how to use exercise equipment. Fitness instructors teach people how to exercise safely.

Professional Athlete

Professional athletes are paid to play a sport. They exercise to stay fit and healthy. They practice their sport. Professional athletes often travel to different cities to compete. Only very talented athletes can become professionals.

compete
to try hard to win a race or a contest

Coach

Coaches teach athletes how to play a sport. They teach athletes the rules of a game. Coaches help players practice. They show players how to work together. Coaches encourage players to do their best.

encourage
to give someone courage
or strength to do their best

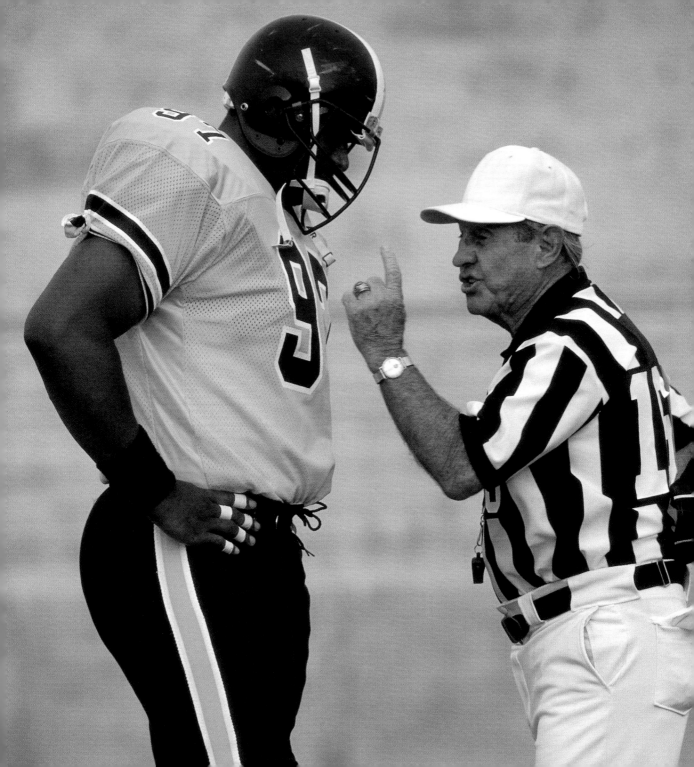

Referee

Referees work during games. They know all the rules of a sport. Referees make sure the players follow the rules. They give penalties to players who break a rule. Referees help make games fair.

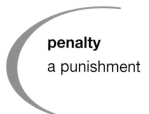

penalty
a punishment

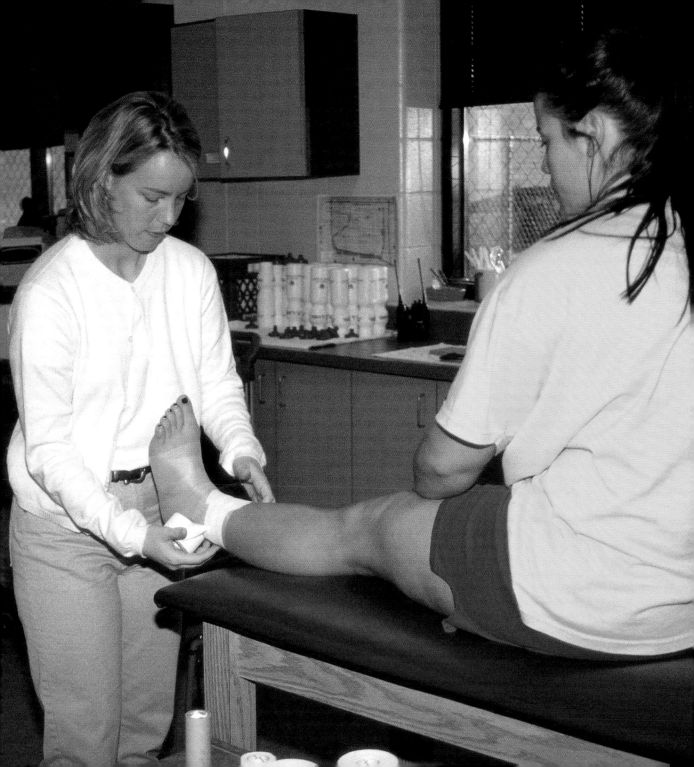

Athletic Trainer

Athletic trainers help athletes stay healthy. They work with athletes to treat and prevent injuries. Athletic trainers learn about muscles, bones, and nerves. They help athletes plan safe exercise programs.

injury
damage or harm to the body

Sports Broadcaster

Sports broadcasters work on TV or on the radio. They may describe a game while it is being played. Other broadcasters report sports news. They read scores and talk about athletes. Sports broadcasters also interview athletes.

interview
to ask someone questions

Preparing to Work in Sports

You can prepare for a career in sports. Exercise and stay healthy. Eat foods that help your body grow. Learn the rules of your favorite sport. Science classes teach you how muscles and bones work. You can learn about fitness in physical education classes.

Hands On: A Racket and Ball Game

You need to know game rules for many sports careers. Make your own equipment and decide on the rules of your new game.

What You Need

2 metal coat hangers
1 pair of nylon stockings (an old pair)
Duct tape or masking tape
1 piece of paper

What You Do

1. Squeeze one hanger hook. This will be the racket handle. Bend the rest of the hanger to form an oval.
2. Cut one leg from the nylon stocking. Carefully pull the stocking leg over the hanger oval. Wrap the leftover stocking around the handle. Tape around the handle and stocking. This will keep the nylon on the hanger and give you a good grip.
3. Repeat steps 1 and 2 to make a second racket.
4. Make a ball by crumpling the piece of paper and wrapping tape around it.

Hit the ball with your new rackets. Practice with a friend. Hit the ball to each other. Make up rules for your new game. Teach your game to a friend.

Words to Know

athlete (ATH-leet)—a person who is trained in or who is very good at a sport

equipment (i-KWIP-muhnt)—the tools and machines needed for an activity

exercise (EK-sur-size)—physical activity that people do to stay healthy

fitness (FIT-niss)—a person's health and strength

interview (IN-tur-vyoo)—to ask someone questions; sports broadcasters interview athletes.

professional (pruh-FESH-uh-nuhl)—getting paid for doing something; professional athletes are paid to play a sport.

Read More

Field, Shelly. *Career Opportunities in the Sports Industry.* 2nd ed. New York: Facts on File, 1999.

Lee, Barbara. *Working in Sports and Recreation.* Exploring Careers. Minneapolis: Lerner, 1996.

Savage, Jeff. *A Career in Professional Sports.* Getting Ready. Mankato, Minn.: Capstone Books, 1996.

Internet Sites

BLS Career Information
http://stats.bls.gov/k12/html/edu_over.htm
Sport Science at the Exploratorium
http://www.exploratorium.edu/sports
Sports Illustrated for Kids
http://sikids.com

Index